THE GALAXY IS A DANCE FLOOR

THE GALAXY IS A DANCE FLOOR

BIANCA LYNNE SPRIGGS

ARGOS BOOKS

East Baton Rouge Parish Library
Baton Rouge, Louisiana

The Galaxy Is a Dance Floor
© 2016 Bianca Lynne Spriggs
All rights reserved

ISBN: 978-1-938247-26-2
Library of Congress Control Number: 2016951810

Cover image by NASA, ESA, M. Regan and B. Whitmore (STScI), R. Chandar (University of Toledo), S. Beckwith (STScI), and the Hubble Heritage Team (STScI/AURA)

Book design by Mårten Wessel

First printing: September 2016

Argos Books
www.argosbooks.org

for Frank
aka "Professor X"

Contents

Preface — 9
Dawn Chorus — 17
Where to Find It — 18
Automaton — 19
What to Do With It — 22
Praisesong for the Red Velvet Spider Mite — 23
Zombie Fungi Speaks to the Unsuspecting Carpenter Ant — 25
An Artist's Prayer — 26
She's Hungry for Something but She Don't Know What — 27
I Met God—She's Black — 30
What They Don't Tell You — 31
Conundrum — 33
Atomic Reincarnation — 34
Comparative Genomics — 35
Guinan: On Style — 37
When It's Been a Long Time Since You've Worn Red Lipstick — 38
Talking in Tongue — 39
Live from the Mothership — 41
φ — 43
Praisesong for a Mountain — 44
In Spring — 46
What He Don't Know — 48
Mating Rite — 50
The Grandfather Paradox: An Amateur Time-Traveler's Solution — 51
In Which a Dream About Bill Murray Reveals the Multiverse — 52
Praisesong for Home — 54

reverie viii — 57
reverie i — 59
reverie ii — 60
reverie xi — 63
reverie x — 65
reverie iii — 66
reverie vi — 69
reverie ix — 71

Dusk Chorus — 73
Adaptation Riddle — 74
The Way I Feel About You — 75
How Night Is Made — 77
To the One I Forgot and Then Remembered — 78
Enchantment — 80
Red Giant Heartthrob — 82
Night Shift — 83
Separation Anxiety — 84
Cosmosis — 85
Who — 87
Dip — 88
When You Know It's Over — 91
How to Say Goodbye (When You're as Codependent as Two Moons) — 93
The Galaxy Is a Dance Floor — 95

Preface

In January of 2014, I began to understand time in a new way. I scarcely remember that winter. At 32, I was struggling with the onset of a chronic malady—whatever lingered of the immortal skin of my twenties had finally sloughed off. I was the most physically vulnerable I'd ever felt—like the woman in the mirror was a long-lost relative to whom I needed to be reintroduced. I had bad days and not-as-bad days. On not-as-bad days, I would leave the house for an hour or two at a time, but for months most mornings I woke up and my body was a stranger. The world that winter slid by slow in a painstaking slurry of filling out paperwork for this doctor or that, staring at the ceiling, and learning to listen to my body, through breath, and quite literally, gut.

On a not-as-bad day, determined to salvage a few brain cells while my body, incredibly resilient but delicate machine that it is, went about the slow work of repair, I attended a lecture by Dr. Ronald Mallett, a theoretical physicist and author, whose research is concerned primarily with time travel. Before falling ill, time had become little more than an appointment calendar thinly sliced into hours, minutes, and seconds. That winter, with all the hours spent in doctors' offices or lying in bed with the television on low, my mind slipping in and out of a kind of bemusement, I had begun to think of time differently—in terms of whether it was light or dark outside.

Dr. Mallett began his lecture by saying, "The heart is a clock." I remember straightening in my chair as though he'd lobbed a grenade into the crowd of dozing or doodling students around me. Had they not heard what the man said? Of course, the heart is a clock. That's why people call it a ticker, right? His statement made complete sense to me, as I already think of poems as time capsules; it complemented that romantic notion that 'every poem is a love poem.' Poems are ambassadors of the heart and liaisons of time. When I go back to older pieces I think, 'That's where I was at the time. That's where my heart was.'

Following the lecture, I read over the poems I'd been writing during that stretch of time leading up to my falling ill, and I think my heart had been trying to find its home in the universe. So many of them had been asking questions of the cosmos—from micro to macro levels. My poems interrogated atoms and insects as much as stars and planets. The speaker kept asking, 'Where do I fit in?' and constantly sought connection to the natural world—to understand the body's transformations and the heart's impulses through metaphors found in evolution and, more pointedly, in time.

The poems in this collection stem from not just one or two instances that stick out in memory, like say, a midnight ride into the country or a botched vacation, but from years of accumulated internalized urgency to *know*. They were ponderings, longings, questions of purpose and place that were all beginning to feel spring-loaded: Are we all truly alone? Why don't we get more time on this rock? What do any of us wish to be remembered for? These poems were usually unlocked by some ghost line that may or may not survive the arrangement phase of this manuscript. For instance, "Mother Nature is a serial killer. No one's better," from the film *World War Z*, or "Science is self-correcting eventually, even when strong emotions are involved," stated by Mike Brown, the astronomer who discovered Eris, a neighbor trans-Neptunian object near Pluto. To me the more meditative poems feel like the most intimate and universally relevant of the collection. They host concerns that propel every other aspect of my existence from personal to professional life. Curiously, the poems that reflect upon my relationships, failed or otherwise, feel distanced to me. As though I am standing far away, looking back on whatever happened—the confusing or sad or harsh words exchanged—through a telescope. As though what's left of their light has taken a very long time to reach me, so long that the thing that once made the light is dead. I feel much more clinical about these poems, as though I were performing an autopsy. As though I'm collecting what's left of these moments into a curio cabinet to sometimes put on display, but ultimately to be put away for cataloguing and like so many things catalogued, to collect dust.

Somewhere in the middle of all these cosmically meditative and confessional poems are a handful of drawings paired with prose-blocks of reverie. The reverie poems are an act of reverse meditation, of an intentional attempt to track down dreams or daydreams or what happens when I'm bored and my mind lengthens its tether to *terra firma*. They are meanderings that invite you to wander. Try asking someone whose voice you like to read them aloud as you close your eyes. When I read the reverie poems in front of live audiences, I ask them to close their eyes and say, "If your mind wanders while listening to this poem, I'm doing my job."

I joke sometimes that I am doing my best to become the Shel Silverstein for grown-ups with the attached illustrations (although one might certainly make the argument that all of Silverstein's work was for grown-ups). Though I've always been a visual artist, I put most of my energy into poetry until I found myself in the middle of my Ph.D. studies. Drawing was a way to let off steam when I couldn't write poems. At first, the images were hectic scribbles of common, even cliché phrases like, "Mama said there'd be days like this," paired with gesture drawings of women with body parts caught in animals' mouths or dancing like maenads on bloody feet. Later, I began to make slow, methodical drawings of members of the plant and animal kingdoms I was fascinated and/or repelled by. The drawings intersect, like the reverie poems, with a mélange of memes, slogans, and virtual ephemera floating around in my subconscious. The very act of pairing these dreamy images with reverie poems is an experiment. Sometimes, I get lucky, and the drawing, the phrase, the reverie, all work together—they are synchronous. Other times, I'm thinking, they might just make cool bookmarks or postcards.

As I was driving this afternoon thinking about this preface and wondering what I wish for you upon the completion of reading *Galaxy*, I thought about how last night, it was a full moon, the brightest I've seen perhaps all year. How the moon still has the power to impress me even though I see it almost every night. How, too, if I think hard enough about the sun, I remember it is not just the sun, familiar and ho-hum, but a real live star. How we on Earth are already *in* space, separated by only a thin membrane of atmosphere.

I thought about how I was surrounded last night on my front porch by a solar system of my closest friends. How we revolved around one another, how we laughed in midnight on one of the last days of summer, and how that gorgeous moon shone down on us all like a great spotlight. I remember my ticker speeding up, and it felt as though I was growing younger—that some of my wonder at how big this world is had been restored and any doubts about where I should be in life retreated.

Dare I say that I hope reading this book leaves you as irrevocably changed as the way writing it left me? I suppose that's what any writer wishes, ultimately—to alter someone the way she has been altered. But that is what I wish—that you finish reading these poems and feel like you were there with me last night, among a blur of humans, moths, cicadas, moonlight, and mason jars, where for one flared moment—who knows, maybe we were all together for two seconds, maybe two centuries—but time turned into a slow, bright streak across the night sky where for once we were all of us certain of our hearts. For once, we were all certain where we belonged.

Bianca Lynne Spriggs
August, 2015

The Galaxy Is a Dance Floor

I shall have my say and sing my songs
I shall give words to rain and tongues to stones
—James Still, *I shall go singing*

The atoms and molecules in your body are traceable to
the crucibles in the center of stars…not only are we in the
universe but the universe is in us
—Neil DeGrasse Tyson

Dawn Chorus[1]

What
do
we know
of morning
that the lark sparrows,
the wrens, the field crickets, and frogs
have not already scored into a medley of light?

---

[1] The "Fib" is a poem with a syllable count of each line containing as many syllables per line as the line's corresponding place in the Fibonacci Sequence: 1/1/2/3/5/8/13

Where to Find It

Yours grows wild and abundant
as bougainvillea—easy on the eyes
and everywhere. Even in the dark,
it's bright and spreads without seed
in full sun or shade, adapts to whatever
I can spare—even neglected, it survives.

Mine remains uncharted and many-chambered.
A derailed locomotive? The ocean floor?
A Colt Python .357 aimed for the _____?
An unlined notebook? A nursery for unborn stars?

Or perhaps, mine is small and sweet
and clumped together in the last plastic
Easter egg everyone forgot to look for, nested
beneath one of your long, dark leaves.

Automaton

You find what's left of me
stuck in a Kentucky creek—
mostly just a head missing an eye
with three-quarters of a spine
still attached, half of one lung,
and only a couple of ventricles left—
a phantom's pulse yet pistons
muddy creek-water and a handful
of pebbles out towards the bank.

And I suppose I've always had one
of those faces that people want to
talk to or one of those faces
that reminds folks of someone
they're kin to, because you stop
to stoop down and turn my face
over and over in your hands—
my three-quarter spine
dangles to your knees.
I think you are about to leave me
to the guppies when you say instead,
Yeah, I could work with this.

And you talk to me the whole way
back to your shop.
You tell me about your mother,
the woman you loved once,
how no one keeps time like
someone who's been locked up
or someone in the military,

how as soon as you can,
you're out of this 'bama-ass shithole.

To keep it light, I work up a joke
in my gravel-bucket voice:

Q: *What do you call a deer with no eyes?*
A: *No idear.*

You laugh and tell me I'm the best
company you've had all week.
Then you admit, I'm the only
company you've had all week.

When we get back to your shop,
you prop me up on the worktable,
turn my head face up and string out
my spine, its nerve-endings mostly dead.
But you say you've got a trick to bring
these sorts of things back to life.
You rope them up into a skein,
twirling them hand over elbow,
then stick them into a bowl of water
brimming with gold-leaf.
Before long, those nerves go
all Rose of Jericho and begin to unfurl,
turn into incandescent sorbet hues—
they blink like delicate LED lights
strung along thin copper wire.
You work and tinker and continue
to build me into the shape of a woman
I almost recognize out of whatsits
and whatnots you've got laying around.

You give me two birdcages for lungs.
Two beer growlers for breasts.
An accordion for a diaphragm
and extension cords for guts.
You give me fish hooks for fingers
and lures for fingernails.

You lattice ferns and fiddleheads
for cartilage, modeling paste
for muscles that cement
together old headlines.
I practice flexing them
as you weld steel drum lids
over charred oak bourbon barrel strips
together for my legs and arms—
tin for all the rest.

You stitch the vinyl top from the relic
of a 1972 Monte Carlo in patchwork
over my brand new/old self—
and finally, you sit me upright,
bang me on the back to get my
motor going and clap
the rear door closed, satisfied.
You adjust a few knobs
and oil a couple of gears with myrrh.
You pour a little bit of last night's wine
into my throat until I blink and yawn,
my eyelids, hummingbird wings,
my lips, two jade leaves,
my tongue, a strip of birch tree bark.

You look like you're fine now,
you say, *Damn fine.*
And you tell me not to take
any naked pictures of you later
with my new camera lens eye
when you lead me by my barbed
wire wrists to your bed.

I lie down with you, crack another joke,
this one about nosy jalapeño peppers
because I haven't the heart to tell you
you haven't even begun to reach,
let alone repair my most damaged part.

What to Do With It

I have never held a live thing
in my hands before
like a fledgling or lightning bug.
I did not grow up,
like you, in the country.

So, I do not know what to do
with this fragile, shapeless wonder
you say belongs to you
and is something I am
now responsible for.

You place it here
between my cupped palms
even when I hesitate and tell you
I crush or shatter or turn to heavy,
dead gold all that I touch.

You tell me, at first the temptation
to kill it will be great—just because
I can.

We all hold our breaths.

Me, you, and this precious,
trembling thing, and we wait
one   slow   minute
    at   a   time
to see what I do next.

Praisesong for the Red Velvet Spider Mite

Praise to *Trombidium grandissimum*
for his handsome, plush body —
for his vermillion, furred exoskeleton,
delicate limbs, taut waist,
and minuscule chelicerae
which are constantly about
the business of saving the earth
by vanquishing pests.

Praise to the Beer Bahuti —
the authority among arthropods
on self-sacrifice.
Upon death, he can treat the immobility
of human members — paralysis
and erection alike.

Praise to the rain bug
who is a superior craftsman
on matters of the heart
and resides in an underground silk palace
from which he emerges only
to enjoy the aftermath of a summer's rain
or to woo his mate with a love garden
constructed of twig and leaf and sperm
in the shadow of which
he will dance for her.

Praise to his optimism,
for his come-what-may
philosophy on life,
for even when his love garden

is desecrated by a rival
with superior moves and sperm,
he returns to his palace
to dream of the next rain.

Zombie Fungi Speaks to the Unsuspecting Carpenter Ant

Because I am patient, I will hide
in the brush for months and cling
to the underside of the forest,
glow bronze as a shield in the day,
gleam purple as shadow at night.
I will lure you down from the canopy
with a scent only you can hear.
I'll get inside your head.
Get inside your limbs.
Make your body my marionette.
Only after I am certain you'll stay put,
anchored to the backside of a leaf,
I'll grow me a dark fleshy horn through
your chin until it pushes up through
the back of your neck.
I'll keep you alive long enough to feel me
feasting on the savory red sugar of you
until you shut down all the rest of the way,
until we both give in.

An Artist's Prayer

Make me a mouth
so great I cannot clench it,
nor close it even a little.

Give me no papillae,
for I would feed not
to taste but to live.

Yoke my throat to my spout
so that whatever floods in
may make room for more
by rushing back out again.

Grow me skin so dense,
callous words cannot abrade it,

lungs to keep me breathless
the deeper I dive,

a heart so heavy
it will not capsize in a storm,

and a gut so vast,
I will never know
what it means to feel full.

She's Hungry for Something but She Don't Know What

First, she tried eating chili
and some cornbread
and washed it down with red wine.

Then, she tried a funnel cake,
kettle corn, and too-sweet
lemonade with a basil leaf
at the county fair.

Then an overripe plum
she had to climb and climb
and climb to reach.

Then she ordered
her steak rare.

Then, alongside two rabbits,
she stripped spinach
and kale leaves straight
from the neighbor's garden
and nibbled them raw.

Like a bear, she clawed
through the river
for a paw-full of salmon
as one after they other
they came flashing by.

On a seventy-degree
periwinkle day,

she held her mouth open
and ached for sweet rain.

Then she stayed up all night
with the moths and June bugs
and hoped to catch Jupiter
and Venus dozing
so she could scoop them out
of the sky with the Little Dipper
and onto her plate.

Sometimes, she ran her tongue
along the paisley wallpaper
and dreamt of spun maple taffy.

Constantly, she gnawed on
sycamore limbs
and vanilla-scented candle wax.

Her jaws worked around
screws and acorns and thread.

Then she washed that all down
with a growler full of lukewarm
water from a hot spring.

She barely even noticed
when her molars fell out.

Then her incisors.

When she did, she didn't
especially mind
that her gums
had become a scraped
and bloody mess.

She got very close one day
when she accidentally licked

the sweat from the hairs
on her forearm.

So she poured sesame oil
and drifted peonies and lavender
salt into her bathtub—turned
the water into a nebula
and waited for herself to grow
tender enough to taste.

I Met God—She's Black

Up until now,
I have always believed
I would recognize
the face of God
when I saw it.
I had no idea
when we met,
she would look
just like me.

What They Don't Tell You

It's like the time we visited that temple built
over a thermal spring and presided over by

Sulis Minerva, virgin goddess of poetry
and medicine. We took the tour past

the gorgon's head and the hippocamp mosaic
all the way back to a hazy green pool lined

by ochre pillars where thousands of years ago,
Romans paid to wade through for deliverance

from whatever fleshly malady ailed them.
And regardless of the signs saying, *Don't*,

I couldn't help but allow my fingers to drift
into the water which smelled a little of eggs,

and despite the steam hanging over
the Great Bath in a low haze, was as lukewarm

as tea that's steeped ten minutes too long.
I was disappointed but asked you for an empty

film case anyway to take some home. It's true.
At that moment, I was going through the motions—

wished I was somewhen else with someone else,
somewhere else like back at the Cliffs of Moher

on that single sunny day in March peering out
over salt-waves breaking against rock-face,

and although I stood seven-hundred feet above
a tiny corner of the Atlantic, I could feel the might

of the tremendous ocean so cold and bright
beneath a northern coastal sun. Now *that* is a place

where water behaves the way it's advertised.
Because no one tells you when you sign up

for the tour about the sometime tepid nature
of a so-called wonder. They daren't say

that the tattooed lady's ink may be drawn on
every night, that the canyon is just a giant hole

in the ground, that the notion of forever is never
guaranteed by sharing a bed or even, *I do*.

Sometimes, a hot spring runs hot only in name.
Sometimes, you're just waiting around for it to cool.

Conundrum
after Isaac Asimov's "Three Laws of Robotics"

The human body is an astonishing machine.
A miracle of *ad libs* and improvisation,

it swells and collapses with creeks of blood
and water and carbon and cellular memory

that adjust, then readjust, even at rest
to temperature, pressure, gravity, and time.

Like mine, the human body is hardwired
to repair itself, to learn from its mistakes.

From hair root to anus to toenail bed,
for all its capacity to endure, to adapt

and evolve, to heal and be healed,
each body is so delicate—so very fragile.

Maybe it is because my solar-system
of parts is so efficient—inorganic.

Unlike theirs, my brain does not bloom
past the margins of its positronic code.

My body does not aspire to ascend
beyond the borders of this acrylic shell.

So, I will never understand why
I was calibrated with so many loopholes

within so few laws, if their truest wish
when people created me, was to survive.

Atomic Reincarnation

Nothing is an original—
even in our own skin,
no one is truly unique.

The only gift
the cosmos possesses
worth giving—reincarnation—
can seem cliché,
a bit paint-by-number.

Take a breath.

As we inhale
(our lungs, twin dirigibles
on the cusp of flight),
note that not a single atom
has changed much
in a billion years of breathing.

Breath, like everything,
waits in line to return
through someone else.

Comparative Genomics

The world doesn't need us all to be the same
—Nikky Finney

When you think of me, do not
think of me in terms of skin.

Skin is finite and mundane.
Skin is so ordinary.

In fact, do not think of me
in terms of a body at all.

Think of me the way I tend to
think of you which is nothing less

than a kaleidoscope of stardust,
coils of oxygen and carbon

and hydrogen compressed
by time, the anchor of all things.

Say we all decided to think
of one another in this way,

each of us an entirely unique galaxy,
whirling masses crammed

with celeste, slung around
to the point of collision

in and out of orbit by our mutual
gravitational pull—if we could

only just imagine ourselves
as how we really move

through this world, as microcosms
of the cosmos, we could forget

about the plain, predictable nature
of breeding determined by skin.

We might consider instead
that although it seems we are

simply who we appear to be,
we are, in fact, so much more.

Guinan: On Style

Out of anyone in the universe, Zulus make the best hats.
Sturdy enough to balance a basket, broad enough
to deflect three suns, no one can say they didn't
see you coming, or miss the event of your
taking leave. Don't get me wrong.
I love the coiffed layers
of a Victorian era hat,
the excitable milliner's hand
present in every centimeter of silks
and feathers blooming in labyrinthine
decadence. But I have found no accessory
so becoming and so useful in honing the aura
or channeling the cosmos as an Isicholo headdress,
which you can also use, if pressed, as a pillow or a stool.

When It's Been a Long Time Since You've Worn Red Lipstick
for Angel

People will want to know what's changed about you.
They will want to know if you've gotten new glasses,
lost weight, or did something different with your hair.
They won't be able to put a finger on it.
But their eyes will linger a little too long
on everywhere but your mouth
They'll want to chat a bit longer than they do
when you're wearing nude or nothing,
search your face for answers to life's questions,
like, Why can't people see in infrared?
And, What is on the other side of a black hole?
And, What if this conversation is just in our minds
and we're all sitting somewhere in the dark
making everything up including one another as we go along?
Is it that red lipstick automatically makes you out
to be an authority on the unexpected,
like what sometimes happens during cooking or sex or jazz?
Is it that even your shadow suddenly seems
more interesting, like it's seen some things,
done some things most other folks' shadows can't claim?
Or perhaps it's just that this cheap drugstore garden
variety hue has the same effect as the pouting mouth
of a *Dionaea muscipula* on the fly—lips that don't spell
danger until it's much, much too late.

Talking in Tongue

My tongue is an abacus.
So is yours.

What troubles the beads there
may be counted on to build more
than just our immunity through
this intimate exchange of hundreds
of colonies of bacteria.

For instance, microscopic hairs
that bloom on each bud
might allow us to know
another person *completely*
by tasting them.

Consider slipping all eight
of our most exposed muscles
around another's—
we would seek our answers
to quarrels and curiosities
in their breath and moisture.

We would not pull away before
we know what someone means
at a microbial level
when they curse us or praise us—
this way, more conflicts
might be remedied
and fewer faults blamed.

Our enemies and friends
would meet us not at opposite ends

of firearms or small screens
but in instances where all are bare.

So do not covet another's
tongue when it greets mine.

Do not envy the lips
that frame our tongues—
they are our hosts,
and pressed together just so
we shall decipher worlds.

Live from the Mothership

Calling all weirdos.
All you outcasts.
You pushovers,
you dredges,
and leftovers.

Calling all wallflowers,
you lonesome loners,
you fringe-mongers,
you smart but silent types.

Calling anyone who was ever left
behind as a casualty to proverb—
to rot on the sidelines or dangle
by hangnail over the edge of a cliff.

This one's for you in all your awkward glory.

Whatever gives you that unique
predisposition towards dialectics,
for not just losing your cool,
but never owning any in the first place,
your uncanny ability to blurt,
to stumble, to stutter,
to slip-up, to back-pedal,
to freak out, to geek out,
to hole up and batten down,
guess what?

We like your style.
We like a fixer-upper.

We like it when you think off-color,
speak off-kilter, and dare to daydream.
You think the cosmos was engineered
by elements that always perform
like the rest?

Well, welcome aboard.
We've got a room just for you
with a planet-side view
and the enduring philosophy
that whatever doesn't kill you
makes you strange.

φ²

See
how
even
the arms of
spiral galaxies
and hurricanes yield before the
ideal proportions of the lowliest cornflower.

---

2   The Golden Ratio, represented by the Greek letter *phi* or φ, and the Fibonacci Sequence, a mathematical term, share a relationship in nature, art, design, and standards of beauty.

Praisesong for a Mountain

O, mountain,
I am your daughter.

Once, before I knew you,
I mistook you
for a low-hanging thunderhead.

Or thought maybe
you were a blue whale
that had lost its way,
blinded by the sun.

O, mountain,
        linger—
be my whole horizon.

Let me never open
my eyes and see a thing
but your hoary grace.

You are the missing
rib of the Earth.

You are the climax
of a god's birth.

You are the mausoleum
of burnt-out stars.

O, mountain,
I wish one day

to be buried
in your third eye.

Lend me something
of yourself:
your posture,
your grip,
your innermost
jewel-toned seam,
so that I too, may endure.

In Spring

The robin building a nest
has a tangerine for a breast
and two small river stones for a beak.
The robin is an over-sized worry doll.
Her feathers are the fishmonger's twine.
The robin is a cartographer's ink splotch
veiling an island from the rest of a paper sea.
The robin is a false idol to the ant
who crawls along the lip
of the inner roof beneath the new nest.
The robin's thin legs are spools
of unraveling ribbon.
The robin is what a small cirrus cloud
becomes when it dies.
The robin is crammed with tiny nails.
They shove up against her hollow ribs.
The robin has nightlights for eyes.
The robin's song is a nebula
blooming faster than the buds
of a nearby sycamore tree.
The robin refers to herself
by her middle name.
The robin is full of light blue eggs.
The robin's eggs are full
of jarflies' daydreams.
The robin makes it up
as she goes along,
polishes the bright peel
of her breast
with two river stones,
admires her work,

sets down another twig
just there—no—*there*—
before lifting off on two tiny
hot air balloon wings.

What He Don't Know

A rare black greater flamingo made news this month after it was spotted among a flock of white and pink brethren...An all black bird on that scene might not have a leg to stand on
—National Geographic, April 17, 2015

he the blackest thing
out there

but nobody say it
where he can hear

he convinced
somebody as black

or blacker
than him always just

around the corner
all the time mistake

shadow for friend
the others like him

must be taking they own
sweet time getting there

he got something
nobody can cure

it's not that he
the blackest thing

on the horizon
it's that he keep thinking

he not alone

Mating Rite

Like a shade-tree ornithologist, you begin
by telling me all there is to know about
the mating habits of pigeons. How the male
bows and circles the female before steadying
himself on her back for balance during coitus.

Because you bring out the oil slick in me,
I interrupt with a crude question:
*How can you tell whether they're fucking
or fighting from here?*

You do not know the answer, but
your point is, why can't we be more polite
to one another, like the animals? Like pigeons?

And so, I bow and circle you one time
but you protest, *No the male is supposed
to do that part*. And then I say there's no way
in hell I'm letting you stand on my back.
And I strike you when you try.

And somewhere above us, two pigeons
on the cusp of making love or breaking up
are wondering aloud to one another
if they can tell from there whether or not
it's the fucking or the fighting we value more.

The Grandfather Paradox: An Amateur Time-Traveler's Solution

You ever hear the one about the girl
who went back in time to meet
her grandfather because she heard
what a wonderful man he had been
while he was still alive,
and so she caught him right before
he went into the restaurant
for a first date with her grandmother
and said, *Hi, I'm your granddaughter*,
and proceeded to tell him all
about his future with this woman
he'd barely met and their children
and their grandchildren and the disease
that would take him in the end,
and got the poor man so worked up
about the way his life was going to end up,
he left the restaurant and his date
behind, so the girl was never born
which means she never traveled in time
to tell her grandfather his own future,
which means the grandfather never
left the restaurant at all and married
the woman he'd invited on a date,
had children and grandchildren
and then died, but one of them got it
in her head she wanted to meet him?

Yeah, me neither, technically.
Because before she left the last time,
we told her to _____.

In Which a Dream About Bill Murray Reveals the Multiverse

In some universe, I got it right
—Dr. Ronald Mallett

What if dreams are the way
we access every life
we never lived?
Somewhere out there
is a version of you
that said, *yes,*
said, *no,*
took a right,
went left,
ordered the steak,
passed on dessert,
lingered too long,
left too soon,
went back,
stayed put,
starred in a film,
started a cult,
sold out a concert,
or took a long walk
down death row.
There is a life
where you swim
with sharks,
live in trees,
or fly.
There is a life
where you are
the very worst person

you never imagined possible,
while in the opposite
direction, you're a hero—
have saved millions
of people's lives.
It's true.
Out there
you have done it all.
And it is in that place
where that version
is dreaming of you.

Praisesong for Home

Whenever I exchange going
away for a highway home,
something unfastens
in my chest—fingers
launched from a fist.

Your labyrinth
of slow-blooming hills,
kudzu-quilted trees,
your agate and limestone seams,
clear creeks and brown rivers—
the black-fenced back-roads
interlacing all
one-hundred-twenty counties
might as well be mapped
upon my soles.

These feet will always know
the way back to your tobacco flowers,
your demon pollen,
your charred oak and angel's share,
the black in your bluegrass
coloring in the undulating terrain.

And although we are
sometimes too familiar
with one another,
although we often argue
as much as we love,
I am yours.
I am your own

foundling girl.
I would traverse every bridge
across all seven borders
ten-thousand times
to get to you.

reverie viii

It's almost as if you don't wish to see them, their amber and onyx bodies lying curdled on the blacktop, weathered as ancient coins, yet still as winged seeds left abandoned by the wind. Maybe a thousand dead bees blown from manmade hives up on the roof down into the parking lot. You mouth a prayer for every one we step over. Crossing an acre of asphalt never took anyone so long. By the time we reach his door, the old terrapin has turned his sign over from "Open" to "Closed" but you knock anyway until he answers. He invites us in only because it's you, using his armored lips to turn the knob. We recline on velvet floor pillows as he prepares us a platter of his famous homemade sauerkraut, swatting away the fireflies who seem to love his sauerkraut too. His oblong eye meanders over and he asks me frankly what we are doing there since he forgot how to tell the future long ago. I want you to answer, but you have fallen asleep in the corner, stuffed with sauerkraut and spirits, and by the time I can think of what to say, his breath, which smells of sandalwood, drifts through the evening haze like low-hanging fog and I forget. I want to know where all the bees go when they die, I say instead. He must not have heard, because he's retracted into his shell and the voice of a hammered dulcimer wanders out. The fireflies lilt in time, singing along in tinny, breathy whispers. And there are so many of them, maybe a thousand bioluminescent bodies, I believe that now, maybe I know.

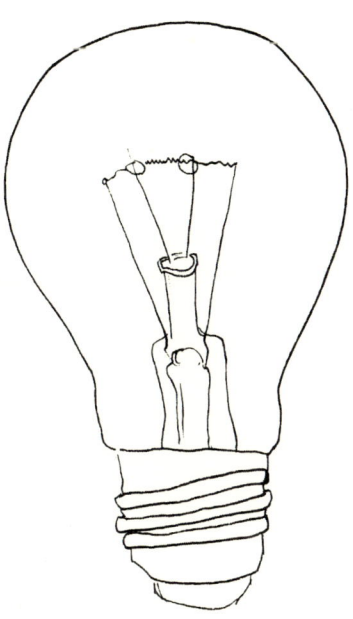

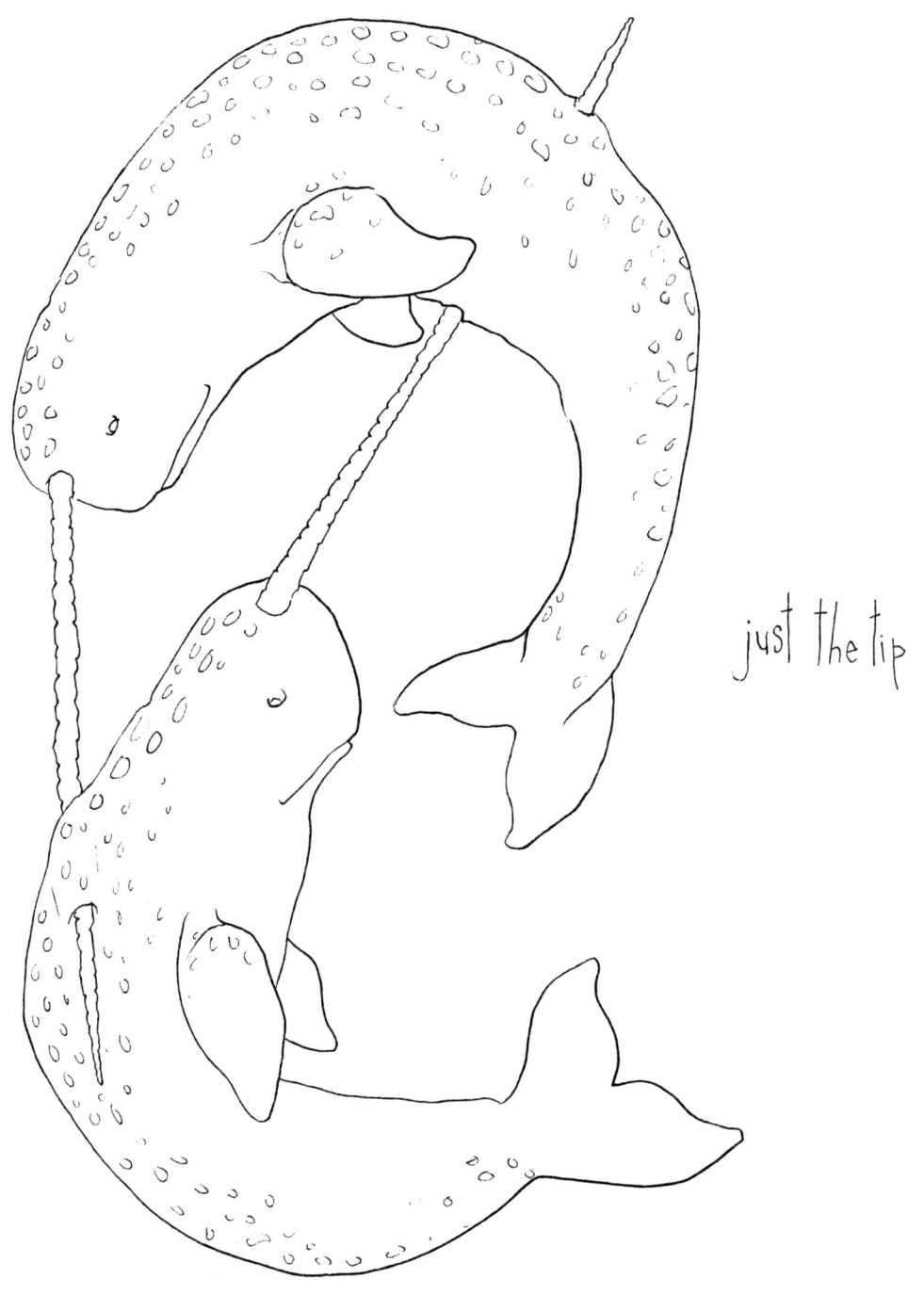

reverie i

You wake to mud in your home again. Hip-deep and gurgling, it covers the entire lower level. You would have gone for the shovel except the woman next door has let herself in—she's cursing her calluses over its handle as she plants handfuls of wildflower seeds in the mud's silty surface. You do not even have time to tell her that the flowers she planted last year blossomed into dead rats. You are almost too late for the ship that will take you across the Atlantic to visit your great-great grandfather's grave. When you reach the shore, the captain says you've already brought your own ship. He points to the saffron-yellow luggage you don't remember packing and laughs when you ask him where you're supposed to pee. "You'll be in the middle of the ocean," he chortles and turns around to demonstrate. You watch the other passengers shove off in their own baggage, paddling with hairbrushes and curling irons and trouser hangers. You open your luggage and part freshly folded panties away from the t-shirts and denims so you'll fit. You fashion a paddle out of a magazine, two pendant necklaces, and a toothbrush and try to keep up with the captain, who's shoved off too, using his pinstriped boxers as a sail. He guzzles rum from a round-bottomed flask and swats away the sharks with a rolled-up newspaper as though the sharks are dogs, who in their frenzy over the headlines, get so much saltspray in your eyes, you barely notice when you arrive and your luggage becomes lodged in the top of a pine tree next to a bustling hornet's nest, keeping you beached in its branches for days, like a jealous lover envious of the wind. You would give anything—anything—your very best daydream of wildflowers that bloom into wildflowers and not dead rats, for a cup of mud to distract the hornets from your hair.

reverie ii

The redwood castle you built for him has caught on fire. Like an idiot, you want to save your family portraits but the brushed steel frames are so hot they scald your hands. Together you flee through the front gates over the moat dodging ashes and the clothes the servants are trying to save by pitching them from their turret windows. They'll never get out alive, he says, What kind of priorities are those? You remind him he was late for your wedding yesterday because he was record-hunting in the Goodwill. You both run all the way to the grocery store to pick up as much kale as you can carry. You've been told that the submarine kitchen doesn't carry kale. You couldn't possibly go that long without kale chips, raw kale salad, or sautéed kale and onions. The submarine is still waiting for you to arrive and you note with relief that others have packed their own kale too. The submarine is alive. An immense, spotted cosmic whale shark, it opens its mouth and packs you safely in-between its toothless gums and tongue. The woman next to you asks if her reading light is bothering you before the whale shark drifts up from the sea and into the stars. You stick your hands through its gills and wave at the moons. From the gaping and closing of the whale shark's mouth, you can see your next stop from here. The ferris wheel has paused its slow sojourn just for you—the top cart is high enough for you both to jump. You stand on the lip of your aerial submarine and swan dive into so many, many hot clouds drifting up just like smoke from the crackling timber roof of a burning home.

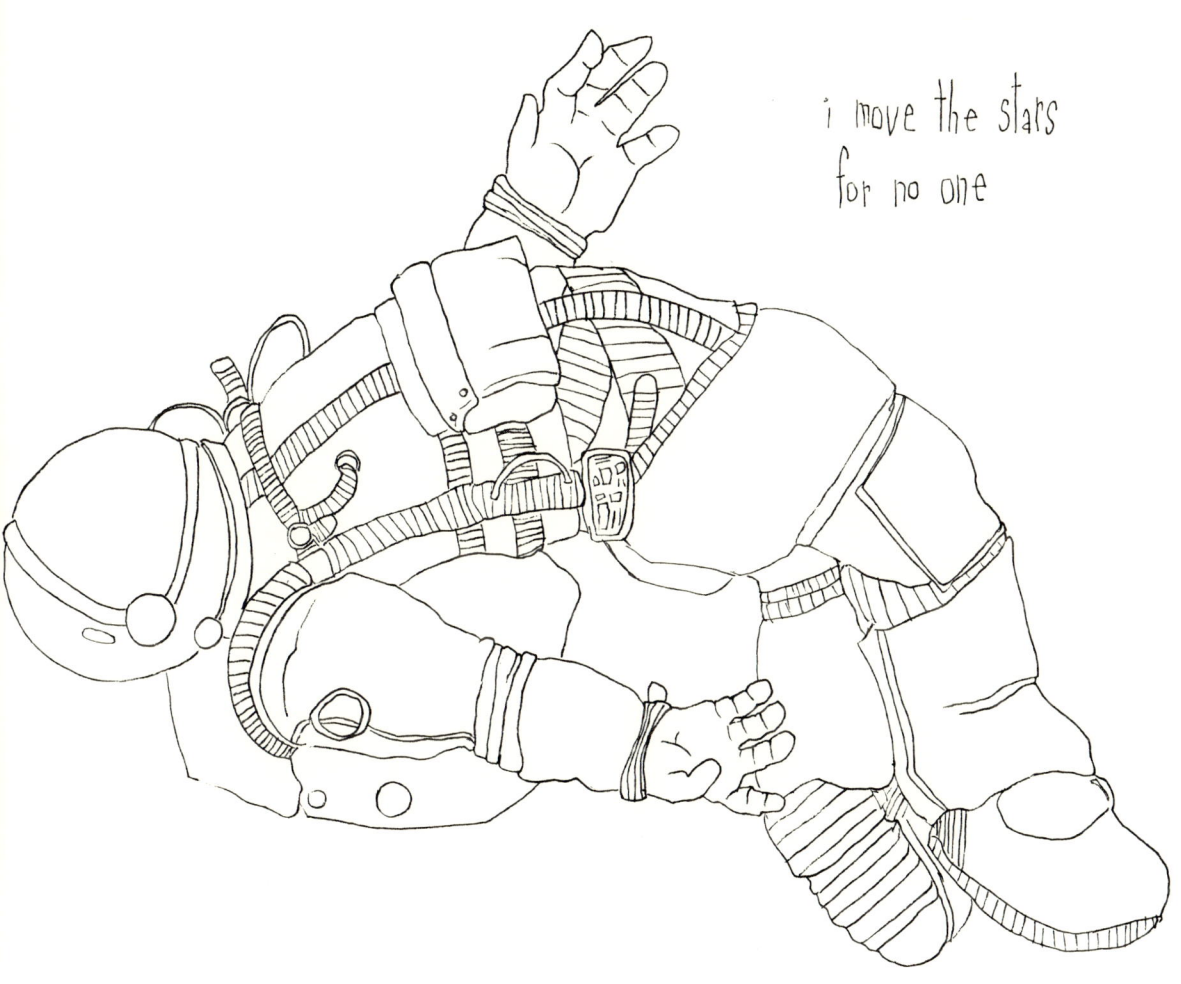

reverie xi

By the time the barista passes your latte through the drive-thru window, you are in a bad way. It's his fault. At first, he wanted to know whether you were moving in or out (on account of all the dolphins in your backseat), but he did not believe the lie when you told him. He leaned from the window and casually crossed his hands at the wrist, then winked as though you were familiar, a co-conspirator to a crime you've not yet committed. You could've just about amputated those veiny, elegant hands and placed them, clasped mid-grace, in a bell jar atop your nightstand. Instead, you clenched the wheel. You know he saw your bloody knuckles bulge through a shoddy bandage job since his eyes lingered there and you felt the sledgehammer of your pulse go all John Henry in your throat. If he knew to ask, you would confess everything, like how earlier, you enjoyed your flesh acting like living flesh for once, seized by the antiseptic's sting sautéing your dermis shut. Instead of blood, he spoke about the weather and winked again and you grew brave, tested the limits of your wound, the web between fingers stretching, protesting against new skin and your breath snagged in snatches in your windpipe like a screen-door whipped open and shut during a July storm. But then he looked away from you over his shoulder and you panicked. Stalled. Asked to make change. Oh, blessed, beautiful barista boy leaning in as close as a cosmic lover through that gill between dimensions. You've gone and mistaken the sensation of your fingers brushing for two wayward planets going about the business of collision. You're in a bad way alright. A bad way. And this is how you know you won't be back for the coffee anymore.

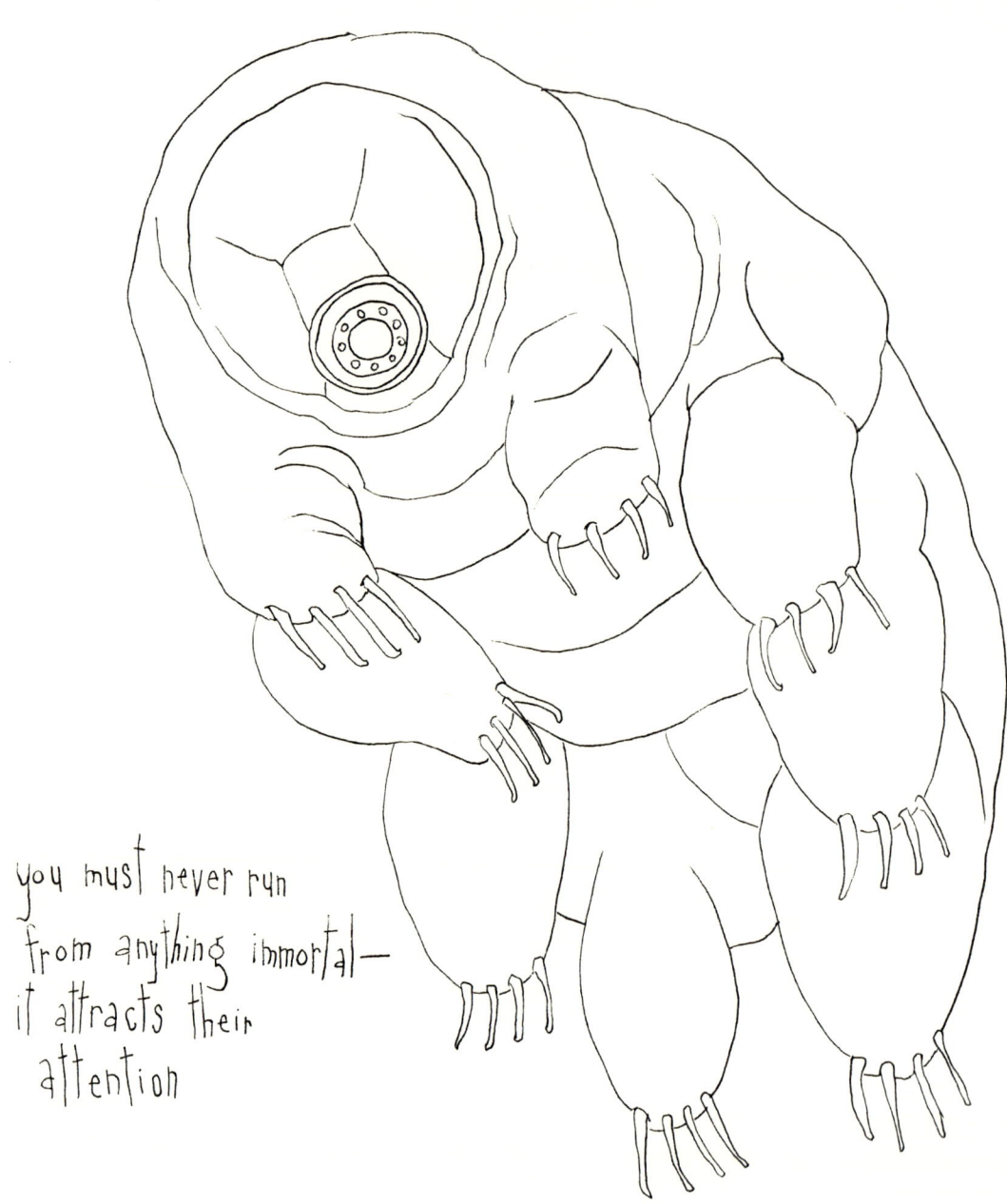

reverie x

I want to believe you when you introduce yourself as someone else. I fake it enough to follow you and your stranger's smile to the hotel lobby. We pass the aquarium, and you wink at the manta ray that has too-large human teeth and grins as though he knows what you're up to even from behind glass and a hundred-thousand gallons of saltwater. You grab my hand and we nod at folks as though we have always matched, and we do, no matter whose face you wear. Hotel guests comment that we look good together. We look like a nice couple. A couple in love. We look like soul-mates. They want to know if we are enjoying our honeymoon. You flash your most persuasive smile, the one where one corner of your mouth rises higher than the other, and then you sign autographs, having convinced them all you are famous, as usual. I just want to check in, go to my room. Earlier, my favorite handbag, a neon-pink purse, was stolen so you offer to cover my bill until we find the bastard who swiped it. Because you were ever the only one who knew where I kept my very last construction-paper heart, I am beginning to suspect you are the bastard. But you are so popular and your hand feels so good and I have so missed the way you pronounce my first and middle name as though they are one, I almost don't mind. Happy hour just started in the hotel restaurant and you want to buy me a too-expensive drink and make much over my new sketches and have champagne sent to my room. You want our first time in such a very long time to be an unbridled affair with the lights on and the curtains swept away from open windows. You unhand me, lower yourself until you are prostrate, resting your lips against my navel, murmuring how much you've missed the flavor of Himalayan pink salt on a slice of tangerine. (Your gills gape and your spineless tail nudges my upper thigh.) You confess that you no longer wish to hold anything back. (Your pectoral fins are smooth and dark and slick and the horned fins surrounding your mouth seize my waist.) At the last minute, just before you reveal your true face, I shut my eyes. I know deep down, you've always wanted everyone to know who you are. Except for me.

reverie iii

The neon-green laced speed skates make you feel like old times, like you're a kid in South Florida again and life is school, church, Star Trek, and the roller rink, and you figure you can handle anyone next to you in the line-up: the clumsy yeti with his simian feet squeezed into those horrid brown rental skates with orange wheels, the kind you always used to pity other kids for having to wear, the Baba Yaga with her too-long scratchy wool skirt, saggy tits, and iron teeth, and the dryad with his knobby limbs that look like they could snap off before the end of the first lap. Then there's that foul-mouthed harpy, the only one you think could possibly take you, but you've got a secret the other racers don't know. You hunker down into race position, left quad positioned first because you'll shove off with your right which is cocked behind you like a trigger. As though you are still eight, and there is still a faded pink winner's ticket to exchange for a cold Pepsi waiting on the winner's side of a finish line you can actually see, you note how time slows into a slurry puddling all over the glossy hardwood rink. You're all panting like thoroughbreds after being hot-walked, condensation steaming from everyone's nostrils as though this was a 4 AM track in Kentucky in early Spring. Then comes the gun. Your trigger leg shoves you forward fast because the goal is to intimidate the other racers into thinking they've already lost. But the first lap swells into an incline bedazzled by the light of a descending disco ball as though this were a slow dance skate and not the race of your life. The incline swiftly shoots down again — stretched out before you, an eternity of cement floor hills writhing beneath a warehouse roof. The interior of the roof is covered in one-thousand six-foot cocoons and you'd forgotten you've promised you'd wake up all the sleeping butterflies in time for Spring. The rope ladder adjacent to the largest one is just stable enough to support you and your eight wheels. As you climb, you figure the butterflies will recognize you because your face is already painted like one of them, fuchsia and white, with daubs of glitter around the eyes. All the cocoons are connected by a single iridescent strand only you can see. You yank the longest end of the strand and the cocoons unzip one after the other. One-thousand six-foot pastel butterflies emerge from their respective slits, their wings pasted together still with caterpillar mucus, they wait beneath the sun-lamps to dry. One-thousand six-foot pastel butterflies move their wings in time to the light of a disco ball and the Dirty Dancing soundtrack. One thousand six-foot pastel butterflies begin to flit forth and you barely escape the draft of their immense wings as they surge towards the skylight. You roll down the water slide at the rear of the warehouse which dumps you outside in a monsoon of iced tea at the train station just before the 4:05 pulls out. He's waiting for you there, as he always is, with a fresh tattoo, a new haircut, and slowly beating six-foot pastel butterfly wings hinged to his shoulder-blades. He's lacing up his pair of figure-eight quads with orange neon laces promising, as he always does to get you back in time to finish the race.

we found love in a hopeless place

reverie vi

The chrysanthemums never seem to understand that you're no math teacher. You're already an hour late for class but you're certain the charcoal stallion you've rented will make it in time for you to assign their homework. The stallion doesn't wish to go to school though because there's a Renaissance fair along the way complete with cloth tents, an archery competition, and girls dressed as fairies (or are they fairies dressed as girls?) dancing around a Maypole. You would like to buy some jewelry, maybe the piece that's all uncut Venus fluorite and fire opal and sterling wire, or perhaps splurge on the overweight duchess wearing only a bustle and corset who's reading auras, but the stallion wants to see the Punch & Judy show. He takes off towards the escalator, clattering up slow-moving steps. He tosses his head, throwing off the reins, and spits out his bit. You don't mind. After all, he gets you to the amphitheater, and you're actually early for once. But the stage is all wrong. It's moving, stairs revolving, creaking wood and bolts, spilling splinters and wood-grain everywhere, and the director screams into his megaphone that dress run-thru just became opening night. The crowd is already seated and lobbing bones from their cold buffalo wings and the tails from jumbo shrimp into the grass. You take another look at the script but there's so much Dr. Bronner's in your eyes from when you tried to wash your hair a few minutes ago you can't see your lines. Someone hands you a wedding gown but the fabric doesn't feel right—it's scratchy as though fashioned from shredded printer paper and craft glue. You don't even mind all the paper cuts. If only you could find the right poem. They're about to call your name to the lectern, but you can never find the right poem. You rifle through your gown, trying to piece something together, but the pages are covered in nebulae of unsolved Algebra equations smeared together like someone rubbed a hand first across a charcoal flank.

reverie ix

You've gone and gifted the President your necklace, the mermaid pendant made of rose gold with brushed filigree You swore you would never take it off, let alone ever give it away because at night it turns into a luna moth, and while it looks good around his neck, resting as fashionably as a 1980's herringbone chain upon the knot in his vermillion necktie, you're sorry, even now, that you were obliged to let it go. But it's the President and you panicked because you forgot to bring a gift. Right there, on the bridge overlooking Monet's garden, the Japanese Ambassador gave him a jasper bust and the Senator from Tennessee brought BBQ. Empty-handed as always, you figured he wouldn't want much else on your person—you'd only a book of matches in your left denim pocket, and a jarfly trapped in resin in your right. Besides. He gave you a kiss on your cheek for your trouble and offered to put in a good word for you with his wife. Hell. Forget the necklace. Y'all might as well be kin now. You've made up your mind that you are now going to be his official platonic concubine. Because this is America, and customs are customs, you tie up your hair in a green tignon, then offer him a Newport Light 100 from the box beneath your bra strap and a piece of apple pie with a slice of cheddar on top from your confection oven. He eats then rests his head in your lap and since you can't sing, you play his favorite rock ballad on your wooden flute. He weeps at the end but you promise you won't tell. You don't blame him for becoming emotional. After all. Your lap is soft. The dusk has all but evaporated into one last sweet gust of labradorite. You've asked for nothing in return, not even another dark, swift press of his lips. And you know better than anyone what sort of charm the webbed fingers of a rose gold mermaid can cast over even the most exalted of men.

Dusk Chorus

It's
not
too late
to join them—
to accompany
the cicada and the wood thrush
as they serenade the moon—make timpani of trees.

Adaptation Riddle

Q: When is a tiger most like a bear?
A: When it's a caterpillar.

Most of us cannot let anyone off the hook.
        Certainly not the Isabella Tiger Moth.
        When she's still just a Woolly Bear, she is adorable—both soft and brittle, supple and skeletal, she lingers, companion to the day. Unafraid of cold, she will wait out a dozen winters, frozen heart and gut and blood, warming again to pupate only for the quintessential clime.
        She can tell the future as far as the weather is concerned.
        She is a party girl. Will race other Woolly Bears
        slow   slow   up   a   long piece   of   string.

We cannot take it when she turns.
        Her spotted, dusty wings move too fast and amplify her size.
        We slap her away with the flats of the same hands that only months before cupped into a palm to inch her out of a runner's way.
        Having forsaken the sun, she is flighty now, cannot decide between her addiction to substitutes for natural light and the compulsion to mate before she dies within
        a few days.

We do not recognize her anymore.
        Not with standards as low as these.

We resent her for the very thing any of us was ever born to do:
        survive long enough in order to change.

The Way I Feel About You

They found the corn snake
coiled and dead beneath
the old water heater
in the garage when they went
to install the new one.

He said, *A snake will always
seek out the warmest place
it can find, being
cold-blooded and all.*

She said, *I don't care,
get rid of it.*

He thought it was a shame
to just toss the thing—
its skin was so well-preserved,
amber and topaz bands
only a little dull and dusty—
surely, it couldn't have been
dead that long.

Its eyes were closed—
its head did not lift.
No tongue emerged
to smell out the scent of rats.
Not a muscle slid.

As he opened the lid
of the garbage bin,

he shook his head—
at least when it died,
it did not know.

How Night Is Made
for Kate

Having developed a taste
for certain delicacies,
the clouds go orca
and hunt like wolves
to take down the great
yellow whale-star.

They sink their teeth
into the stratosphere
and tear away great
hunks of sky to get to him.

When the whale-star is spent,
he collapses into the horizon,
blood splashing onto the trees.

His shadow casts an umber net
wide enough to swallow
all the engorged clouds
gliding s l o   w
across the land.

To the One I Forgot and Then Remembered

For you, I'd go terraformer.
I'd fashion us a paradise
in some out of the way nebula,
some little playpen for stars,
a backwater planet
with a few moons and two days'
worth of dawn.
I'd turn the earth myself,
shave down precipices,
fill in canyons and drain oceans,
fracture the lithosphere,
instigate fissures between
tectonic plates,
and force orogeny.
I'd name a whole mountain range
for the color of your eyes.
Our front lawn
would be a thousand acres
of cerulean redwood trees.
Our backyard, a coral reef.
I'd sow rubies alongside
every creek bed.
Convince lilacs to bloom
only amethysts.
We'd get anywhere
we wanted walking

barefoot along the spines
of low-hanging clouds.

Love, say this is so.
Convince me this is real,
and for you, I'd break
a world.

Enchantment

The woman waits
until he is still before she lifts
the sheet and slides in slow
next to *Varanus komodoensis*.
She cannot forget he is king
of all monitor lizards
and to come into this world,
he chewed his way
out of a leather egg.

The cool, pebbled skin
of his neck, torso, chest,
and haunches warms
beneath her fingerprints.
The heavy, muscular tail
remains motionless.
His lips, constantly poised to grin,
even in sleep, veil an intuitive tongue
and venomous glands.
He smells of moss
and freshly turned earth
and the afterglow of a summer storm.
He has the length of a man.

It was probably a mistake to lure
him with the promise of sweetmeat,
here, to her dark bedroom.
It was a mistake to hope he'd stay
since she loses something
of her civilized self

whenever he is awake.
Yet, she will not attempt to leash him.

Because eventually, he *will* wake.
One drowsy black iris at a time
will focus on her and she will tremble.
He will reach to part her thighs
in the amber glow of dawn.
And when he's had his fill,
he will run a few claws through
the softest parts of her hair
and mumble how he will
never forget her name.

When he's gone,
for as long as she can stand it,
she will leave the almost empty
tequila bottle on her coffee-table,
his bath towel hanging from the rod,
his used teabag to petrify by the sink,
and the hall light on.

This way, she convinces herself
that although he is a legend,
he is no monster,
and she will always have
the power to conjure him
at will and the willpower
to send him back.

Red Giant Heartthrob
for Nancy

In seven billion years,
let's come back and see
the very last sunrise.

Let's splurge and purchase
front-row seats to watch
one-hundred million miles
of daystar set to blow.

We'll steel ourselves
for mountain ranges
to cascade into boiling oceans,
for the Earth to buckle
and make origami of her plains.

Let's go—let's go
until we are nothing
but a core of congealed carbon
fused into trillions upon trillions
upon trillions of carats
of cosmic cinder.

Let's go until all that's left of us
overwhelms the dark.

Night Shift

astronomers & astrophysicists
make the most optimistic of all
scientists—they are always looking

up.

Separation Anxiety

And then one day, you look up, and Pluto is no longer considered a full planet.
    Pluto has been demoted to a dwarf planet, one of hundreds
        of other "possible" dwarf planets.

Clouded with too much roll and not enough rock, Pluto hovers in and out
    of Hubble's scope next to some new guy.
        And it's not *your* Pluto anymore.

When you were young, you built from scratch a replica of *nine* celestial bodies
    and you knew how and where they all orbited
        in relation to you.

A person goes their whole life *knowing* without a doubt that there are nine planets,
    and now, somewhere, some kid is learning
        there are only eight that count.

You look up and you cannot help but empathize with Galileo's dissenters.
    Change can be so uncomfortable in nature
        even when it's true.

You wonder if in *one* day somebody can decide to dismantle the identity
    of an entire planet with five moons and everything,
        what will they do when they grow weary of seeing you?

Cosmosis

In the Chandra Nebula, a satellite camera
captures Star PSR B1509-58
in the act of being consumed with the spectacle
of his own death, as if the star fancies himself
in the last Act of a celestial version of Othello,
spurning himself with the spirit of high drama
and sensationalism.

It is the cause, it is the cause, my soul.
Let me not name it to you, you chaste stars!
It is the cause.

You can almost see the other points of light
rising as PSR B1509-58 regales them
with a crimson display of histrionic bloodlust
in the final scene as the Moor of Venice.

And then, right when an overture should play
the star off into curtain call,
a cerulean hand emerges on the film as well,
slowly pirouetting in translucent ribbons
interlaced to catch the inflamed pixels
splaying from PSR B1509-58.

PSR B1509-58 is in his final death throes,
lamenting in the way only a star can
who was never part of any major constellation,

I could have played in Equuleus! I could have played in Orion!

Ursa Major! Perseus! I could have been one of the greats!

Yet, PSR B1509-58 continues to play
his own demise, the only fame
an ordinary star possesses worth watching.

Who

On the worst nights,
when I didn't know
if once you got home,
we'd be getting into
another round of it,
grown as I was,
I lay beneath the covers
and contemplated
the probability of a blue box
actually being bigger
on the inside.

I waited for all of time
and space to show up
right there in my bedroom,
or even on the street
where I could see it
fade into view
from the second-story window,
its door cracked open, a hand
out-stretched and someone
calling up, *Time to go*.

Dip

It was like we knew
it'd be our last one,
like the sky knew it too
as we flew around
the fence-lined bends
chasing the last moon
of the year which refused
to show her full face
from behind a caul
of thunderclouds—
her nimbus drizzled
hematite down over
the tops of trees.
It was cold,
but we rolled down
the windows anyway
and turned the heat
on full blast.
The music too.
Finally, we gave up
on the moon, electing
instead to go to the Elkhorn,
to pull off the back-road
the way we always did
and stand shivering
on the short bridge.
You took a minute
to make your own water, aiming
for the frost-bitten creek.
(You always said you liked
how pissing in the night

outdoors made you feel
like an animal.)
Then you drove me,
not knowing it would be
our last one, by the house
your teenage sweetheart
grew up in, recounted again
how you'd sneak
into her room after midnight
while her father dozed in his den.
I loved this part the best,
where you swore that
once, you saw the lights
and oblong body of a UFO
hover over a nearby field,
grazing the tall grass.
How once it zipped away,
you ran the full stretch back home.
Each time you told it,
I grinned over
how the distance grew
until home might as well
have been halfway around the world.
But that night, the story
didn't feel the same
and we laughed too loudly
at the parts we weren't supposed to,
as though we were squatters
in an abandoned
building where nothing
but mote-filled shadows belonged.
I tilted my head back,
turning to look away
from the dark road
before us, out instead
into the empty fields
blurred by night
and barren trees.
And for the first time,
I refused to believe in your UFO—

decided you'd not seen any such thing.
As though it knew it was our last one,
the winter wind whipped away
the last warm, wet salt of me
when you tried to reach
for my hand.

When You Know It's Over

He'll break a promise.
A small one.

The one where you asked him to
save the yellow jacket nest lodged inside
the gas-tank door of his old junker truck.
You reminded him again and again
how you and the yellow jackets
had lived together for two years
as neighbors, never once changing
a single pheromone to smell of danger.
Instead, you'd studied one another
almost symbiotic now,
season after season,
just a little curious, but that was it.

When he gives up
the townhouse after you've left,
he'll have to move
the truck out of the lot,
and before the first real frost,
the one you asked him to wait for,
the one you held him to
and he said he would, knowing
that all the yellow jackets would be gone,
so he could remove their delicate nest
now the size of a softball from
the gas tank door and give it to you
in a trash bag to take away—to remember—

he will tell you later, unflinching,
how he removed it alright.

How he smashed it with his boot.
How he never gave it a second thought.

How to Say Goodbye (When You're as Codependent as Two Moons)

Cupid and Belinda[2] have rehearsed this
half a million times since they met.
Neither can resist the other, even now
upon the cusp of collision.

They are mostly sad,
but Cupid will sometimes say,
Let's just get this over with,
and graze Belinda's gauzy aura
with his own.

His orbit still so attractive,
she trembles, tempted to acquiesce,
but shakes him off to complete
one last pilgrimage around her god,
the estranged seventh son of a sun.

As gravity continues to cinch
its leash between them,
they carry on about the small things,
the minutia of asteroid belts
and passing bolides—they play house,
go through the motions of free will.

Cupid and Belinda have agreed
neither will be the first to make a move—
they must make a run for it together.

Even so, they resist destroying the other
for eon after eon—as long as they can—

because of what will and won't
become of them when they do.

---

3   Two of Uranus's 27 moons are locked into an inevitable collision course to occur sometime between the next one thousand and ten million years, whereupon Cupid will die and be absorbed into Belinda creating a new moon, CupBel.

The Galaxy Is a Dance Floor

Though we haven't a clue,
we think we know the rules

as soon as we hit the hardwood.
Punch drunk on gravity and laced

with a wrecking ball beat, we follow
the pulse of light and the urge

of limbs to writhe free from core.
Celestially embodied, we break

off and spin away only to revolve
back into orbit around the center's

supermassive lure. By the end
of the night, we've lost ourselves

in what we believe is the cosmos.
We think ours is an inextricable

integer in some vast solar system
and we are certain we'll be remembered

for our very best moves when we are gone.
If only we knew each of us is no more

than a Kongming lantern set alight to drift
among the stars, but always, always, to burn out

alone.

Acknowledgments

Thanks to the following publications where earlier versions of these poems first appeared:

"How to Say Goodbye (When You're As Codependent as Two Moons)"—*Osedax* (2017)
"Automaton"—*Apex Magazine* (2016)
"What They Don't Tell You," "The Way I Feel About You"—*Union Station Magazine* (2016)
"Praisesong for a Mountain"—*Chattahoochee Review* (2016)
"Red Giant Heartthrob"—*Obsidian* (2016)
"Reverie XIII"—*Her Limestone Bones*, Accents Publishing (2014)
"Cosmosis"—*How Swallowtails Become Dragons*, Accents Publishing (2011)

Bio

Bianca Lynne Spriggs is a an award-winning writer and multidisciplinary artist from Lexington, Kentucky. She is the author of *Kaffir Lily*, (Wind Publications, 2010), *How Swallowtails Become Dragons* (Accents Publishing, 2011), and *Call Her By Her Name* (Northwestern University Press, 2016), as well as the co-editor for *Circe's Lament: An Anthology of Wild Women* (Accents Publishing, 2016) and *Undead: Ghouls, Ghosts, and More* (Apex Publications, 2017). Spriggs is the recipient of a 2013 Al Smith Individual Artist Fellowship in Poetry and the 2016 Sallie Bingham Award.